AF584436

World Heritage Sites in Australia

Kakadu, Uluru, Kata Tjuta and more...

Northern Territory and Western Australia

Ellen Millen

First published 2017 by
Redback Publishing
PO Box 357 Frenchs Forest NSW 2086
Australia

978-1-925630-12-1

Author: Ellen Millen
Editor: Jane Hinchey
Designer: Redback Publishing

Original illustrations © Redback Publishing 2017
Originated by Redback Publishing

Printed and bound in China by Leo Paper

Acknowledgements
Abbreviations: l—left, r—right, b—bottom, t—top, c—centre, m—middle
We would like to thank the following for permission to reproduce photographs: (Images © shutterstock) p5b Hung Chung Chih, P20 Maurizio De Mattei, p25 EQRoy,

Every effort has been made to contact copyright holders of any material reproduced in this book. Any omissions will be rectified in subsequent printings if notice is given to the publisher.

Contents

Page 6 World Heritage Sites and UNESCO
Page 9 Sustainability and World Heritage Sites
Page 10 Heritage Organisations in Australia
Page 14 Kakadu National Park, NT
Page 20 Uluru, NT
Page 22 Kata Tjuta, NT
Page 24 Australian Convict Site Fremantle Prison, WA
Page 26 Shark Bay, WA
Page 28 Purnululu National Park, WA
Page 30 Ningaloo Coast, WA
Page 32 Glossary
Page 32 Index

What Makes a Place Special?

All around the world, people show that they value special places in different ways. Sites that are special because of their history, beauty or spiritual significance are preserved so that they do not deteriorate and will still exist for future generations to enjoy. Special places can be important for just one person, a group or community, or for everyone in the world.

Various groups in communities look after their special places in different ways

UNESCO

UNESCO identifies World Heritage places around the world.

Governments

Governments at all three levels in Australia make laws and regulations to identify, preserve and protect special places.

Community Groups

People in a local area often join together in groups to protect special places from destruction. Protest groups in Australia have been successful in the past in helping to preserve places of natural and built heritage. Many people donate their time and skills to help maintain special places such as bushland sites or historic buildings.

Individuals

Individuals who care about special places can look after them by being careful not to do anything that might degrade a site. Avoiding littering, not lighting campfires in the bush on days of high fire danger, and not engaging in graffiti or other unlawful activities all help to preserve special places.

Special Places

Make your own list of special places. The list could include homes, shops, parks or even a room or a special spot underneath a tree.

- Why are these places special to you?
- Will they still be important to you in the future?
- Are your special places important to anyone else?

Think about the places that are important just for you. Are they the same places that your friends or family think are special? What makes a place special to you?

World Heritage Sites and UNESCO

UNESCO is a division of the United Nations. It assesses sites around the world for their cultural and natural value to humanity. In 2017, there were 1,052 World Heritage Sites worldwide. Nineteen of these are in Australia.

> *"To be included on the World Heritage List, sites must be of outstanding universal value and meet at least one out of ten selection criteria"*

World Heritage Convention

The work on cataloguing World Heritage Sites began in 1972 as a result of an international treaty known as the World Heritage Convention. Australia was one of the first nations to become involved. Once a World Heritage Site has been determined, the country in which it exists must preserve and protect that site. Countries which have signed the treaty can work together to preserve sites that are of international importance.

World Heritage Committee

The World Heritage Committee is a group of some of the member countries of the United Nations. Committee members serve a fixed term. The role of this committee is to administer all matters relating to World Heritage Sites listings. Australia has been a committee member on a number of occasions.

UNESCO's World Heritage Mission

- To encourage more countries to sign the World Heritage Convention and contribute sites.
- To encourage countries to set up management plans for their sites.
- To provide emergency and technical assistance.
- To encourage local populations to become involved in preserving sites.

Threats to UNESCO World Heritage Sites

World Heritage Sites that are in danger of destruction are listed by UNESCO in their List of World Heritage in Danger. None of the sites in Australia are currently on this list. This is due to the diligent work undertaken by governments and individuals in Australia, and the high regard that Australians have for their heritage sites.

Threats to sites on the List of World Heritage in Danger currently include:

- Natural disasters like earthquakes or cyclones
- Wars and civil conflict
- Uncontrolled expansion of towns and cities
- Unchecked tourist development
- Neglect
- Lack of funds
- Pollution
- Poaching

In 2017, there were 55 sites listed by UNESCO as being under threat.

World Heritage Fund

Member nations contribute to the World Heritage Fund. Countries that do not have the financial resources to care for a site can apply for funding to assist them.

Saving World Heritage Sites

UNESCO has been involved in saving some of the world's most iconic sites and their surroundings, including:

- Angkor, Cambodia
- Dubrovnik, Croatia
- Giza Pyramids, Egypt
- Delphi, Greece
- Abu Simbel, Egypt
- Venice, Italy

What is a Plan of Action?

Before setting out to protect a heritage site, it is important to have a Plan of Action. This plan will help to make the conservation process efficient and therefore more effective. Whether the heritage site or special place is being cared for by a government, a community group or an individual, their Plan of Action can include the following points:

- Set a definite goal.
- List the things that may stop this goal being achieved. Examples are a lack of funds, unfavourable weather or groups which oppose the goal.
- List all the activities that will be required to achieve the goal.
- Set priorities for which activities are the most important.
- Decide who will do the work required to achieve the goal.
- How will the goal affect other people who are not involved?
- Where will the funding come from?
- Work out a timetable for achieving the goal.
- Have regular reviews of the Plan of Action and make changes to it if necessary.

How a Heritage Listing Affects Communities

When a place receives a heritage listing, either from UNESCO, a government body or a private organisation, the listing can result in both positive and negative impacts on the community.

Positive Effects

- The heritage site is preserved for future generations.
- Owners of heritage listed buildings can apply for grants to help maintain them.
- Nations can apply for funding from UNESCO to care for their World Heritage Sites.
- More people know that the site exists.
- The world community can encourage nations to continue preserving their sites.
- Heritage sites produce a positive economic effect through their impact on tourism.

Negative Effects

- Indigenous people living in the area may be stopped from using it as a food source and as a place to perform traditional ceremonies.
- People may be stopped from using land as a holiday campsite.
- People cannot usually take pets with them into natural heritage areas.
- Farmers who have been grazing livestock in an area may be stopped from doing this.
- Houses that receive a heritage listing cannot be demolished or changed. Owners need special permits for any work on their building.
- Access to some areas in natural heritage sites may be restricted.
- The construction of roads and buildings is either not allowed or restricted.

Sustainable Tourism in World Heritage Sites

Tourism is a significant activity in World Heritage Sites. UNESCO advises countries with World Heritage Sites on sustainable ways to manage tourism.

At Australian World Heritage Sites, sustainable management of tourism includes:

- Building boardwalks or raised viewing platforms in natural areas so that tourists do not damage the environment when walking through it
- Closing sites, allowing them to regenerate
- Controlling the provision of sewerage and garbage services
- Restricting or forbidding access to sensitive areas
- Banning pets
- Educating the public on the value of the sites and how to behave when visiting them

Sustainability and World Heritage Sites

- Natural sites are involved in carbon storage in the form of trees and plants.
- Natural sites contribute to the water cycle and to climate regulation.
- Natural sites contribute to maintaining the Earth's biodiversity. This is important for the health of humanity, since many of our new medicines come from research undertaken into the properties of rare plants.
- UNESCO reports that climate change is likely to affect World Heritage Sites.

Q&A

Q. Can a place ever stop being a World Heritage Site?

A. Yes. The Arabian Oryx Sanctuary in Oman and the Elbe Valley in Dresden are no longer listed after failing to meet the requirements for preservation of the sites.

Yosemite National Park

Heritage Organisations in Australia

The Role of Governments and Heritage Councils

UNESCO is not the only organisation that determines whether places have heritage significance. The three levels of government in Australia, federal, state and local, also compile their own listings of important places. There are many more sites and items on these lists than on the World Heritage List for Australian places. Each state and territory has a Heritage Council which advises government on matters relating to heritage places.

Historic Shipwrecks Program

Shipwrecks more than 75 years old are protected by legislation. No items can be taken from them and divers must not move any part of the ship. Severe penalties apply. Shipwrecks that contain the remains of people, unexploded ammunition on warships or other sensitive contents may have access to them restricted. Anyone who discovers an historic shipwreck must report it to the government department responsible for shipwrecks in the relevant state.

Famous Australian Shipwrecks

- HMS Sirius in Slaughter Bay, Norfolk Island is one of the ships of the First Fleet
- Japanese midget submarine M24 from the Second World War is in the sea off Sydney

Overseas Special Places For Australia Listing

This listing is created by the Australian government.

- ANZAC Cove, Gallipoli
- Kokoda Track, Papua New Guinea
- Howard Florey's Laboratory, Sir William Dunn School of Pathology, UK

National Trust

The National Trust has organisations in each state and territory. Their aim is to preserve and promote Australia's cultural heritage. The National Trusts own over 300 heritage places.

Australian Institute of Architects

The Australian Institute of Architects keeps a list of notable buildings of cultural heritage across Australia. A building's importance is based on its aesthetic, historic, social, spiritual or technical value to the community.

Heritage Homework

Some school buildings around Australia are listed on state heritage registers. Is your school one of them? Are there any heritage listed school buildings in your area?

Shipwreck

ANZAC Cove

Australia's 19 World Heritage Properties (2017)

1. Australian Convict Sites
2. Australian Fossil Mammal Sites (Riversleigh / Naracoorte)
3. Fraser Island
4. Gondwana Rainforests of Australia
5. Great Barrier Reef
6. Greater Blue Mountains Area
7. Heard and McDonald Islands
8. Kakadu National Park
9. Lord Howe Island Group
10. Macquarie Island
11. Ningaloo Coast
12. Purnululu National Park
13. Royal Exhibition Building and Carlton Gardens
14. Shark Bay, Western Australia
15. Sydney Opera House
16. Tasmanian Wilderness
17. Uluru-Kata Tjuta National Park
18. Wet Tropics of Queensland
19. Willandra Lakes Region

Kata Tjuta National Park

All World Heritage Sites in Australia are protected by law under the Environment Protection and Biodiversity Conservation Act 1999.

NORTHERN TERRITORY

Kakadu National Park, NT

Kakadu National Park is one of two World Heritage Sites in the Northern Territory. Located about 240 kilometres east of Darwin, Kakadu is the largest national park in Australia. Some of the ancient rocks in the park date back to over 2,500 million years ago. Noted for the diversity of its flora, fauna and landscapes, Kakadu encompasses mangroves, coastal plains, sandstone cliffs, wetlands and forests. Each of these areas has its own array of wildlife, some of which is not found anywhere else. Kakadu has had a World Heritage listing since 1981.

Wildlife

Plants and animals in Kakadu have evolved adaptations to allow them to survive in the park's varied habitats.

- The green plum has waxy leaves to reduce water loss during the dry season.
- Eucalypt trees have a deep root system to allow them to access sources of water underground.
- The Kakadu plum loses its leaves in the dry season to conserve water.
- The Cooktown ironwood produces a poison that deters animals and termites from eating it.
- Resurrection grasses appear to be dead in the dry season but will revive quickly after rain.
- Snake-necked turtles burrow into the mud as the water dries up.

The Importance of Mangroves in Kakadu

Mangroves provide a vital habitat for many species of aquatic and land animals. They also stabilise the coastline, reducing damage to delicate ecosystems from storms and waves. Mangroves have evolved special ways to deal with having their root system submerged in salt water, a condition that would kill other trees. These adaptations include:

- Roots that grow upwards into the air instead of down into the soil.
- The ability to pump salt out of their leaves and roots.

Escarpments

The sandstone cliffs in Kakadu are called escarpments. They are up to 300 metres high. The land that is now Kakadu was once submerged under a sea, with the cliffs at Twin Falls and Jim Jim forming the shoreline. Nourlangie Rock and Ubirr were once islands in this ancient sea. The stony escarpment is now the location of the waterfalls, gorges and rock art sites which make Kakadu such a popular tourist destination. While the surface of the stony area may be dry and hot, the deep gorges and pools provide microclimates that support a lush variety of plants and the animals that feed on them.

Coastline and Tidal Flats

The coastline of Kakadu provides nurseries for many species of fish. They spend their juvenile stages in the safety of the mangrove swamps, and move out to the open sea when they have grown. The mangroves also provide nesting places for birds during the wet season. The beaches offer egg-laying sites for flat-back turtles and the sea-grass beds just off the shore support dugongs. Crocodiles also live in these northern parts of Kakadu, and attacks on people near waterways have occurred.

Wetlands

About thirty species of migratory birds visit the Kakadu wetlands each year. They come from Siberia, China and Japan and depend on the presence of a pristine environment for their continued existence. Australia has agreements with the governments of China and Japan to ensure that the breeding grounds of these migratory birds are preserved.

Ranger Uranium Mine

The Ranger Uranium Mine is within the boundaries of Kakadu. In consultation with the Aboriginal custodians of the land, the mine management will restore the site as their mining operations are concluded.

Bininj Mungguy People

Kakadu is on the traditional lands of the Bininj Mungguy Aboriginal people. In their Dreaming, the wonders of Kakadu were created by their ancestral and spirit figures.

Warramurrungundji, Mother of the Earth, created the waterways and wildlife. She taught her children how to live on the land and, when she rested after this task, she became a large rock. This is now her Dreaming site.

The Rainbow Serpent is usually a female spirit in the Kakadu Dreaming. She is always present in the land and likes water and quiet areas. If disturbed, she can create natural disasters to show her displeasure.

The rock art of Kakadu is mostly found in the rocky escarpment. Some of the older art was created by ancestral spirits to teach future generations about laws.

Archaeologists have dated the rock art to 20,000 years ago, and human habitation to 50,000 years ago. The Bininj Mungguy people trace their ancestry to the time of the creation of the land by the ancestral spirits.

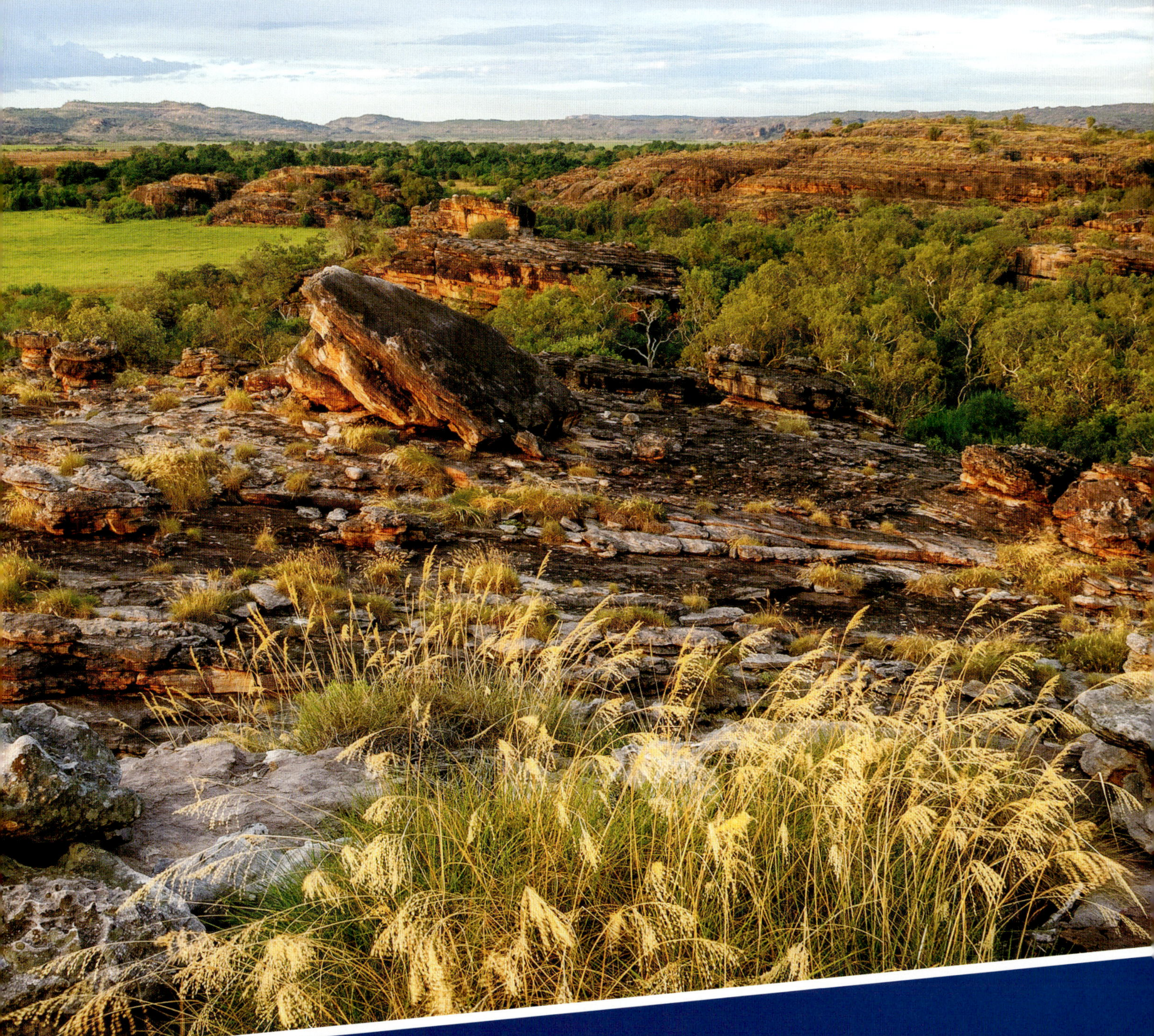

Six Seasons

Kakadu's traditional custodians recognise six seasons, based on the climate, the landscape and local animal behaviours.

December to March:	Gudjewg (monsoon season)
April:	Banggerreng (stormy season)
May to June:	Yegge (cool season)
June to August:	Wurrgeng (cold season)
August to October:	Gurrung (hot and dry season)
October to December:	Gunumeleng (pre-monsoon season)

Kakadu in the Past

The environment and heritage were not always treated with the respect they receive today. Kakadu's beautiful wetlands were once called swamps and thought to be dangerous, disease-ridden places.

During the 19th century, many people believed that nature was only of any value if it contributed to their needs. This idea continued right up until the late 1900s.

Kakadu remains largely unspoiled. There has been little impact on it from European colonisation activity, which has included mining and cattle grazing. The crocodiles, insects, heat and regular flooding in the wet season all deterred European settlers from staying there.

Kakadu in the Future

Threats to Kakadu in the future will come from:

- Cane toads
- Climate change
- The demands resulting from increased tourism
- Feral animals such as the Asian water buffalo and feral cats
- Waste products from nearby mining
- Natural weathering of rock art

UNESCO reports that future improvement to the Kakadu site would result from changing the unnatural straight line boundaries to ones that follow more natural features. Inclusion of the Coburg Peninsula might also be considered in the future.

Think About This

How do water buffalo, cane toads and feral cats damage the Kakadu World Heritage Site?

How do they affect native plants and animals in Kakadu?

ULURU-KATA TJUTA NATIONAL PARK, NT

The Uluru-Kata Tjuta National Park has been a World Heritage Site since 1987 due to its natural and cultural value to Australia and the world.

Uluru, NT

The Pitjantjatjara and Yankunytjatjara (Anangu) Aboriginal people are the traditional custodians of Uluru and Kata Tjuta. The magnificent rock formations represent the lives and works of the creation ancestors and spirits. The first European to find Uluru was William Gosse in 1873. He named it Ayers Rock.

Uluru is over 300 metres high and is thought to extend two kilometres underground. It measures more than nine kilometres around the base. Alice Springs is 450 kilometres away. To accommodate the thousands of tourists who come to see and experience Uluru, the town of Yulara has been developed nearby.

Methods for Conserving Aboriginal Rock Art

The rock art around Uluru was painted using ochre and other natural substances. The same artistic symbols are repeated across the region and include circles, dots, U-shapes, animal tracks and paths. The paintings were made for spiritual purposes and to teach the next generations of people about law and the ancestral creation spirits.

The rock art is protected today using a variety of methods:

- Viewing platforms are built for visitors to use. This discourages them from touching the art or adding graffiti.
- Rangers remove insect and bird nests.
- Silicon drip lines are placed around paintings to stop water running over the surface.
- Penalties will be imposed on people who deface rock art in a national park.

Mala (Rufous-Hare Wallaby)

The ancestors of the Aboriginal people in the area were the Mala people. Their descendants have a responsibility to protect the Mala. This wallaby was extinct on the Australian mainland, but a group of them has been reintroduced to the area around Uluru and is now thriving.

Handing Back Uluru

On 26th October 1985, Uluru was handed back to its traditional custodians by the Australian government. The national park is jointly managed by the Australian Parks and Wildlife Service and its Aboriginal owners.

Kata Tjuta, NT

Kata Tjuta is a group of dome shaped rocks about fifty kilometres away from Uluru, within the Uluru-Kata Tjuta National Park. The name means 'many heads' in Pitjantjatjara. The tallest dome of Kata Tjuta is 546 metres high, which is taller than Uluru. Between the domes are gorges and secluded, deep valleys. The two walking tracks around the domes are The Valley of the Winds Walk and the Walpa Gorge Walk. Kata Tjuta is an Anangu men's site and is therefore a special place with spiritual significance.

The Geology of Kata Tjuta

The rocks of Kata Tjuta were harder than those which have weathered away on the surrounding plains, leaving the red domes exposed. Cracks in the great domes then became wider over millions of years, resulting in steep-walled gorges.

Advice for Tourists

The Uluru-Kata Tjuta National Park is in a desert environment. If the temperature rises too high, the tourist walks are closed for public safety. People need to take water with them and to dress appropriately for a walk in a desert.

Uluru and Kata-Tjuta in the Past

The Anangu people cared for the desert and semi-arid parts of their land so that it would continue to provide future generations with food and water. Sustainable land practices included careful burning to encourage new plant growth, maintaining water springs and not overusing any food source.

European settlers found the conditions in the area very difficult. However, they mined for minerals and engaged in cattle farming where there was enough artesian water.

Threats to Uluru-Kata Tjuta National Park

- Uluru is a sacred place and visitors are asked not to climb it. Those tourists who do climb it often leave rubbish behind or take pieces of the rock, desecrating it.
- There are resources in the ground that are sought by miners. Mining in the site is currently prohibited.
- The increasing popularity of 4WD vehicles causes damage to the park where drivers go off-road.

The explorer Ernest Giles found Kata Tjuta in 1872 and named it The Olgas.

WESTERN AUSTRALIA

Australian Convict Site - Fremantle Prison

Why Are Australia's Convict Sites Important?

Australia was founded as a convict colony, a place where Britain could send its thousands of prisoners. Convicted for a variety of crimes, including theft, assault or causing political disturbances, the convicts provided the labour which allowed Australia to grow into a bustling colony of Britain. They included women, men and children from the age of nine years old. The last convicts arrived in 1868, ending 80 years of transportation. Australia has eleven early convict World Heritage Sites.

What Do the Convict Sites Reveal About the Past?

- The types of housing people lived in.
- The difference in housing and places of work of different classes of people.
- The harshness of the punishments for criminals.
- Many jobs that once existed are now replaced by technological inventions.
- Technology has replaced domestic animals in transport and for ploughing fields.
- We can observe how some building methods have not changed very much at all.

Fremantle Prison

Building of this colonial prison began in 1852 to house the convicts who were transported to Western Australia. The layout was based on the Pentonville Prison in England and it was the most modern design of the time. The role of prisons was changing in Britain, and this influence extended to Fremantle Prison as well. Prisons were becoming places of reform as well as punishment.

Fremantle was chosen as the prison site because the convict labourers were needed to help build the shipping port there. The prison buildings retain many of their original features, allowing us to see how colonial prisoners lived and worked.

Convicts in Western Australia

Western Australia was founded in 1829 without any convicts. However, free settlers found there were not enough workers, so they persuaded the colonial government to start accepting convicts from Britain so there would be a source of cheap labour. Ten thousand male convicts arrived in Western Australia from 1850 to 1868, and the Fremantle Prison was the first place most of them were housed after they arrived.

Management of the Heritage Site

- The Fremantle Prison site is now a tourist attraction, welcoming visitors who want to see how convicts lived during the 1800s.
- There are exhibitions, tours and special programs for visits by school groups.
- Tourism contributes to the preservation of the site, since the buildings have to be well maintained to keep them safe for use by visitors.

Shark Bay, WA

Shark Bay is at the most westerly point of the Australian mainland. It has been on the World Heritage list since 1991.

Some of Shark Bay's heritage features:

- The stromatolites in Hamelin Pool are an ancient life form that existed on earth billions of years ago. They are often called 'living fossils'.
- The seagrass beds in the bay are the largest in the world and feed 10 per cent of the world's dugongs.
- Shark Bay protects a number of species of endangered and threatened animals: Burrowing Bettong, Rufous Hare Wallaby, Shark Bay Mouse, Western Barred Bandicoot, Banded Hare Wallaby, Green Turtle, Loggerhead Turtle, Manta Ray.
- Shell Beach is covered in a layer of shells up to ten metres deep.
- 100,000 visitors to Monkey Mia each year have the rare experience of hand feeding wild dolphins that swim up to them at the beach.
- Humpback whales visit Shark Bay on their migration along the coast.

Threats to the World Heritage Site at Shark Bay

- feral animals
- effects of livestock
- tourism
- recreational boating
- salt and gypsum mining
- fishing and aquaculture
- climate change
- bushfires on the islands in Shark Bay
- future expansion of the desalination plant which provides fresh water

Irrabuga Mia is the Malgana Aboriginal name for Monkey Mia. 'Mia' means home in Malgana, but no one knows for certain why the term 'Monkey' was chosen for the name of the tourist beach where dolphins come to visit.

Stromatolites

Purnululu National Park, WA

The Purnululu World Heritage site is a remote, semi-arid wilderness in the Kimberley region. The outstanding natural feature of the Purnululu National Park is the Bungle Bungle Range. The eroded sandstone of the Bungle Bungles creates steep gorges where fan palms flourish, and waterfalls and pools support a vast range of wildlife in an otherwise dry and hot environment.

The unusual landscape of the Bungle Bungles includes thousands of large mounds coloured with red, orange and black bands. These rocks are 350 million years old. The black bands in the rocks are the remains of ancient single-celled creatures that lived millions of years ago. They are called cyanobacteria, and they were the first forms of life to appear on Earth.

Purnululu National Park has been on the World Heritage List since 2003.

Threats to the heritage site

- Pollution washed into the area from mine sites
- Adjoining areas used for livestock
- Invasion by feral cats, donkeys and cane toads
- Climate change

Management of the heritage site

- Park rangers live in the area
- The park is closed during the wet season
- Aircraft must use only set flight paths to reduce noise
- Controlled burning of the grasslands

Ningaloo Coast, WA

The Ningaloo Coast of Western Australia has been on the World Heritage List since 2011.

Aboriginal History of the Ningaloo Coast

Archaeologists have found a shell necklace in the area that is 30,000 years old. Shell middens, fish traps and burial grounds are all evidence of the ancient association the local Aboriginal people have with the Ningaloo Coast site. The traditional custodians are the Jinigudjira and Baiyunga peoples.

The Ningaloo Coast's heritage features are:

- the diversity of its marine life
- the wildlife living in its underground caves
- the underwater scenery and the striking, arid landscape
- the Ningaloo reef and its marine life
- whale sharks that gather in the Ningaloo waters in the largest numbers known anywhere in the world

Management of the Ningaloo Coast heritage site involves controlling any potential threats to its heritage status. These threats could come from:

- activities on Australian Defence Force land in the area
- tourism
- overuse of groundwater which would affect underground cave systems
- feral animals and plants, both on land and on the reef
- commercial fishing
- offshore mining

Animals in Ningaloo's Underground Caves

The limestone caves of the Ningaloo Coast are home to the unique descendants of animals that once lived on the ancient supercontinent called Pangaea. These include a blind eel that has evolved with no predators in the cave. Because of this, it has never developed fear of being touched, and will allow scientists to pick it up when they are studying it.

Do you keep guppies as pets?
Guppies are small, colourful fish that people often have in fish tanks. Never release them into wilderness areas, particularly the water in caves. The guppies can destroy the natural habitat and the precious wildlife in the cave waters.

Glossary

adaptations	evolutionary changes to help a living thing to survive
aesthetic	relating to beauty
aquaculture	farming of aquatic animals
artesian water	underground water source
desecrate	treat a sacred place without respect
escarpment	cliff at the edge of a plateau
heritage	thing or characteristic that is handed down from previous generations
microclimate	climate in a very small area
shell middens	places where the debris from eating shellfish and other food has accumulated over time
species	separate groups of animals or plants
transportation	sending convicts from Britain to the Australian colonies
UNESCO	United Nations Educational, Scientific and Cultural Organization

Index

animal adaptations 14
Australian Aboriginal Culture 15,16,20-22,27,30
Australian Institute of Architects 10
Bungle Bungle Range 28
Hamelin Pool 26
heritage councils 10
Monkey Mia 26,27
National Trust 10
plan of action 8
Ranger Uranium Mine 15
shipwrecks 10

Visit these websites to find out more about Australia's World Heritage Sites and special places

whc.unesco.org/en/list
www.environment.gov.au/heritage